STECK-VAUGHN
ACHIEVE
New York State
English Language Arts
8

Harcourt Achieve
Rigby • Steck-Vaughn

www.HarcourtAchieve.com
1.800.531.5015

ACKNOWLEDGMENTS

Project Authors   Carol Alexander, Judith Herbst, Estelle Kleinman, Marlene Roth, Sandra Shichtman, and Marren Simmons

Photo Credit   P. 41 © Melvyn D. Lawses; Papilio/CORBIS

Grateful acknowledgment is made to the following authors, agents, and publishers for permission to use copyrighted materials. Every effort has been made to trace ownership of all copyrighted material and to secure the necessary permissions to reprint. We express regret in advance for any error or omission. Any oversight will be acknowledged in future printings.

From *The Adventures of Huckleberry Finn* by Mark Twain, originally published 1884.

"A Proper Place" from DARKER ENDS by Robert Nye. Copyright ©1969 by Robert Nye. Reprinted by permission of Farrar, Straus and Giroux, LLC.

"The Delicate Balance," from *Our Global Greenhouse* by April Koral. Copyright ©1989 by A. Koral. Used with permission of Franklin Watts, a division of Grolier Publishing Company, 90 Sherman Turnpike, Danbury, CT 06816. All rights reserved. Now a division of Scholastic Library Publishing.

"The Monster as Clark Kent," from PRESENTING ROBERT CORMIER by Patricia J. Campbell, G. K. Hall, © 1989, G. K. Hall. Reprinted by permission of The Gale Group.

From "The Raven" by Edgar Allan Poe, originally published 1845.

"Ohio Town Finding Future in Historic Civil War Past," from an article in *Newsday*, December 23, 1998. Reprinted with permission of The Associated Press.

"Rocking-Horse Winner," by D. H. Lawrence. From *Complete Short Stories of D.H. Lawrence*. ©1955.

"Invictus," by William Ernest Henley. From *Modern American Poetry and Modern British Poetry*, edited by Louis Untermeyer. Published by arrangement with the Estate of Louis Untermeyer, Norma Anchin Untermeyer c/o Professional Publishing Services Company. This permission is expressly granted by Laurence S. Untermeyer.

The New York State Testing Program in English Language Arts is published by CTB/McGraw-Hill. Such company has neither endorsed nor authorized this test-preparation book.

ISBN 0-7398-9435-8

© 2005 Harcourt Achieve Inc.

All rights reserved. No part of the material protected by this copyright may be reproduced or utilized in any form or by any means, in whole or in part, without permission in writing from the copyright owner. Requests for permission should be mailed to: Paralegal Department, 6277 Sea Harbor Drive, Orlando, FL 32887.

Steck-Vaughn is a trademark of Harcourt Achieve Inc.

4 5 6 7 8 9 10   1413   12 11 10
4500246500

Achieve New York State
Contents

New York State English Language Arts Standards 2
To the Student 3

Modeled Instruction
    Reading 1 4
    Reading 2 12
    Listening 20
    Writing 29
Test-Taking Tips 32

Practice Test for New York State English Language Arts
Book 1 33
    Session 1 35
Book 2 49
    Session 1 51
    Session 2 61
Answer Sheet 77

New York State English Language Arts Standards

Standard 1: **Students will read for information and understanding.**
Students will write for information and understanding.
Students will listen for information and understanding.

- Understand stated information
- Draw conclusions and make inferences
- Make basic inferences
- Use text to understand vocabulary
- Use knowledge of structure, content, and vocabulary to understand informational text
- Compare and contrast information

Standard 2: **Students will read for literary response and expression.**
Students will write for literary response and expression.
Students will listen for literary response and expression.

- Determine use of a literary device
- Determine meaning of a literary device
- Interpret theme
- Identify author's point of view
- Interpret characters
- Interpret plot
- Recognize how author's language use creates feelings
- Interpret setting

Standard 3: **Students will read for critical analysis and evaluation.**
Students will write for critical analysis and evaluation.
Students will listen for critical analysis and evaluation.

- Use critical analysis to recognize point of view
- Use critical analysis to evaluate information
- Use critical analysis to evaluate ideas
- Distinguish between fact and opinion
- Identify author's techniques
- Identify author's purpose

To the Student

This book will help you prepare for the New York State English Language Arts Test. The first part of the book lets you practice on different kinds of questions you will see on the real test. It also gives you tips for answering each question.

The second part of the book is a practice test that is similar to the New York State English Language Arts Test. Taking this test will help you know what the actual test is like.

The New York State English Language Arts Test includes questions about reading, listening, and writing. It will ask you to write about what you have listened to and read. Test questions will help measure how well you understand the skills outlined in the New York State Learning Standards.

Kinds of Questions

Multiple-choice Questions

After each multiple-choice question are four answer choices. For the Modeled Instruction part of this book, you will circle the letter next to the correct answer. For the Practice Test, use the separate Answer Sheet and fill in the circle that has the same letter as your answer. Remember to pick the choice that you think is the best answer.

Open-ended Questions

These questions will not give you answer choices. You will need to write out your answers. There are two kinds of open-ended questions:

- **Short-response Questions**

    These questions will be scored on reading and listening comprehension. They will not be scored on writing.

- **Extended-response Questions**

    This question has its own symbol. When you see this symbol next to a question, you know this question will be scored on reading and listening comprehension and on writing. Be sure to plan before you write and check your writing for correct grammar, punctuation, capitalization, spelling, and paragraph organization.

Modeled Instruction: Reading 1

DIRECTIONS: Mark Twain's fictional characters often live near the Mississippi River. Huckleberry Finn is one of Twain's best-known characters. Read this excerpt from *The Adventures of Huckleberry Finn.* Then do Numbers 1 through 7.

The Adventures of Huckleberry Finn
Chapter 1
by Mark Twain

You don't know about me without you have read a book by the name of *The Adventures of Tom Sawyer,* but that ain't no matter. That book was made by Mr. Mark Twain, and he told the truth, mainly. There was things which he stretched, but mainly he told the truth. That is nothing. I never seen anybody but lied, one time or another, without it was Aunt Polly, or the widow, or maybe Mary. Aunt Polly, Tom's Aunt Polly, she is—and Mary, and the Widow Douglas, is all told about in that book, which is mostly a true book, with some stretchers, as I said before.

Now the way that the book winds up is this: Tom and me found the money that the robbers hid in the cave, and it made us rich. We got six thousand dollars apiece—all gold. It was an awful sight of money when it was piled up. Well, Judge Thatcher, he took it and put it out at interest, and fetched us a dollar a day apiece, all the year round—more than a body could tell what to do with. The Widow Douglas, she took me for her son, and allowed she would sivilize me; but it was rough living in the house all the time, considering how dismal regular and decent the widow was in all her ways; and so when I couldn't stand it no longer, I lit out. I got into my old rags, and my sugar-hogshead again, and was free and satisfied. But Tom Sawyer, he hunted me up and said he was going to start a band of robbers, and I might join if I would go back to the widow and be respectable. So I went back.

The widow she cried over me, and called me a poor lost lamb, and she called me a lot of other names, too, but she never meant no harm by it. She put me in them new clothes again, and I couldn't do nothing but sweat and sweat, and feel all cramped up. Well, then, the old thing commenced again. The widow rung a bell for supper, and you had to come to time.

victuals = food

When you got to the table you couldn't go right to eating, but you had to wait for the widow to tuck down her head and grumble a little over the victuals, though there weren't really anything the matter with them. That is, nothing only everything was cooked by itself. In a barrel of odds and ends it is different; things get mixed up and the juice kind of swaps around, and the things go better.

After supper she got out her book and learned me about Moses and the Bulrushers; and I was in a sweat to find out all about him; but by-and-by she let out that Moses had been dead a considerable long time; so then I didn't care no more about him; because I don't take stock in dead people.

Pretty soon I wanted to smoke, and asked the widow to let me. But she wouldn't. She said it was a mean practice and wasn't clean, and I must try to not do it any more. That is just the way with some people. They get down on a thing when they don't know nothing about it. Here she was a bothering about Moses, which was no kin to her, and no use to anybody, being gone, you see, yet finding a power of fault with me for doing a thing that had some good in it. And she took snuff too; of course that was all right, because she done it herself.

Her sister, Miss Watson, a tolerable slim old maid, with goggles on, had just come to live with her, and took a set at me now, with a spelling-book. She worked me middling hard for about an hour, and then the widow made her ease up. I couldn't stood it much longer. Then for an hour it was deadly dull, and I was fidgety. Miss Watson would say, "Don't put your feet up there, Huckleberry;" and "don't scrunch up like that, Huckleberry—set up straight;" and pretty soon she would say, "don't gap and stretch like that, Huckleberry—why don't you try to behave?"

. . . I went up to my room with a piece of candle, and put it on the table. Then I set down in a chair by the window and tried to think of something cheerful, but it warn't no use. I felt so lonesome.

The stars were shining, and the leaves rustled in the woods ever so mournful; and I heard an owl, away off, who-whooing and the wind was trying to whisper something to me, and I couldn't make out what it was, and so it made the cold shivers run over me. Then away out in the woods I heard that kind of a sound that a ghost makes when it wants to tell about something that's on its mind and can't make itself understood, and so can't rest easy in its grave, and has to go about that way every night grieving. I got so down-hearted and scared I did wish I had some company.

Go On

1 Which sentence from the story introduces flashback, the literary technique that interrupts a story to portray an earlier episode?

- **A** "I never seen anyone but lied, one time or another, without it was Aunt Polly, or the widow, or maybe Mary."
- **B** "Now the way the book winds up is this: Tom and me found the money that the robbers hid in the cave, and it made us rich."
- **C** "Then for an hour it was deadly dull, and I was fidgety."
- **D** "Then I set down in a chair by the window and tried to think of something cheerful, but it warn't no use."

Tip: To find flashback, look for the portion of the passage that takes place in a more distant past. Look for words or phrases showing that a character is telling a story from the past. Skim the first few paragraphs of the passage, looking for phrases that mean the same as "here is a story about what happened."

2 Which statement best expresses the main idea of the passage?

- **F** Always try to do your best and work very hard.
- **G** Help others but do it for the right reasons.
- **H** Realize that people's ways of life can be quite different.
- **J** Tomorrow's victories can happen because of today's effort.

Tip: To find a main idea, think about what the passage means or what lesson you might have learned by reading it. Skim the passage, trying to sum up in a single sentence what you have read. Focus on what Huckleberry seems to have learned in his dealings with the Widow Douglas and Miss Watson.

3 Huckleberry dislikes living with the Widow Douglas because he

- **A** thinks her life is too structured and proper
- **B** must do too many chores
- **C** does not like the names the widow calls him
- **D** thinks the widow does not like him

Tip: When a question asks you to understand a character's feelings, skim the passage to find examples of issues that make him or her feel a certain way. Reread paragraphs 3 through 6 to find what Huckleberry is asked to do and not do at the Widow Douglas's house. Consider how he describes the issues.

New York State English Language Arts Standards
1. **(2) Read for literary response and expression.** Determine use of a literary device.
2. **(2) Read for literary response and expression.** Interpret theme.
3. **(2) Read for literary response and expression.** Interpret characters.

6 • Modeled Instruction

New York State

4 After running away, why does Huckleberry return to the Widow Douglas?

- F to join Tom Sawyer's band of robbers
- G to show that he is sorry
- H to return to an easy life
- J to follow Judge Thatcher's orders

Tip: Understand what makes a character do certain things by skimming the passage for his or her explanation. Reread the second paragraph to find what Huckleberry says about why he returns to the Widow Douglas.

5 This story is told by a

- A first-person narrator
- B second-person narrator
- C limited narrator
- D omniscient narrator

Tip: Remember that most stories have either a first- or a third-person narrator. If the narrator uses the pronoun "I" to write about himself or herself, the story is an example of first-person narration. If it is told in third-person, decide whether the narrator knows all things (omniscient) or whether his or her knowledge is limited to just a few characters or events.

6 Which of the following best helps the reader sympathize with Huckleberry's loneliness?

- F "I heard that kind of a sound that a ghost makes when it wants to tell about something that's on its mind and can't make itself understood..."
- G "Pretty soon I wanted to smoke, and asked the widow to let me. But she wouldn't. She said it was a mean practice and wasn't clean..."
- H "Then for an hour it was deadly dull, and I was fidgety. Miss Watson would say, 'Don't put your feet up there, Huckleberry.'"
- J "She put me in them new clothes again, and I couldn't do nothing but sweat and sweat, and feel all cramped up."

Tip: When asked to sympathize with a character, try to understand his or her sorrow or trouble. Reread the last paragraph of the passage, looking for clue words such as "mournful" and "down-hearted."

7 Huckleberry's "old rags" are a symbol of his

- A lack of money
- B need for comfort
- C past adventures
- D love of history

Tip: Remember that symbols are physical objects that represent ideas. Skim paragraph 2, looking for clue words that show how Huckleberry feels while wearing the old rags.

Go On

New York State English Language Arts Standards
4. **(2) Read for literary response and expression.** Interpret plot.
5. **(2) Read for literary response and expression.** Identify author's point of view.
6. **(2) Read for literary response and expression.** Recognize how author's language use creates feelings.
7. **(2) Read for literary response and expression.** Determine use of a literary device.

DIRECTIONS: The following article describes a colony of English settlers in America. Read "The Lost Colony of Roanoke." Then do Numbers 8 through 14.

The Lost Colony of Roanoke

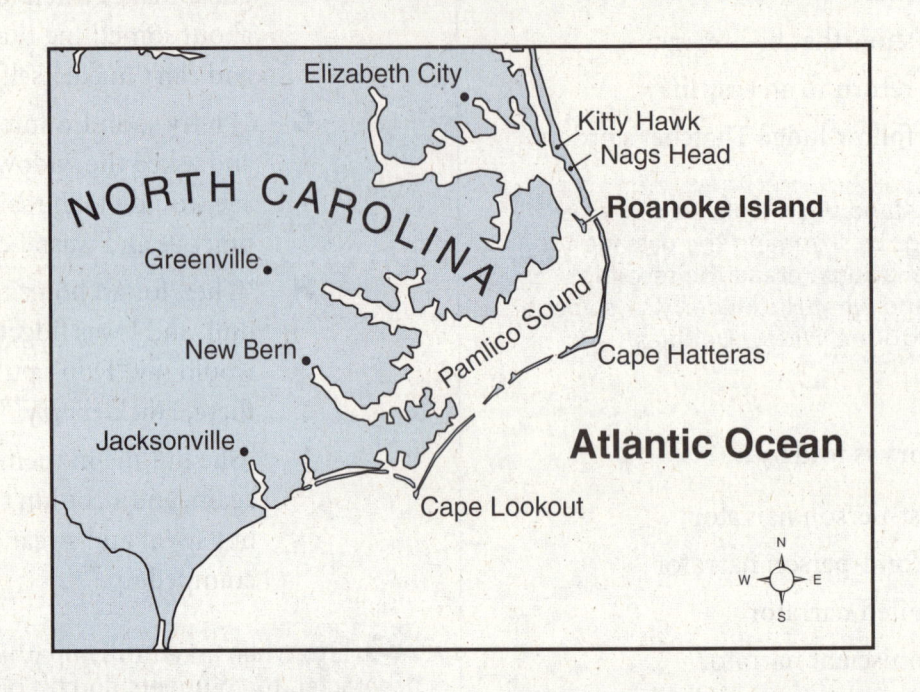

More than thirty years before the Pilgrims landed at Plymouth Rock, an English colony was founded on Roanoke Island. The date was 1585. Elizabeth I had given permission to Sir Walter Raleigh to establish a colony along the shore of what is now North Carolina. Raleigh immediately sent his cousin, Sir Richard Grenville, and a small band of 108 men to the wilds of America to see if they could make a go of it. The settlers suddenly found that if they wanted something, they had to make it themselves. Trees had to be chopped down, all the bricks for their houses had to be formed and baked, and a forge had to be built so they could manufacture nails.

Friendly Native Americans welcomed the colonists at first, but opposing values and different ways of life made relations difficult. The two groups clashed over minor things. Eventually, a tricky peace prevailed, and before long, the Indians were planting crops and making fish traps for the colonists.

But soon they were almost completely dependent upon the Native Americans' practical skills and on supply ships from home. There were lean times between the planting of spring crops and the late summer harvest. The colonists began to pine for the comforts of England. As hunger and hardships took their toll, the settlers grew more and more intolerant of the Native Americans' unfamiliar ways, and by June of 1586, the groups were at war.

Into this somewhat risky situation, Sir Walter sent a second group of colonists a year later. When the travelers stepped ashore, they found a few homes still standing but needing repair. They found that thanks to the efforts of an Indian named Manteo from the nearby island of Croatoan, peace had been reestablished and the settlers were left to try again.

But as before, the big problem was a lack of provisions. Just a week and a half later, one of the ships headed back to England. On board was Governor John White, whose daughter had just given birth to Roanoke's first citizen. In the meantime, war broke out against Spain, and all of England's ships were pressed into service. Eventually, White got a ship back, but not until three years later. What would he find when he returned to Roanoke?

As the ship approached one of the outer islands, the crew could see smoke rising through the trees but found no sign of any people. The following day, they set out for Roanoke, but one of the boats capsized, and it was nightfall before they were able to try again. Foundering in the pitch-black sea, they saw a light and rowed toward it, but they were afraid to attempt a landing in the darkness. Instead, they anchored the boat, blew a trumpet as a signal, and sang English songs at the top of their lungs. No one answered.

When they reached the island the next morning, they found that the colony was gone. All that remained were a few smoldering trees. There were no people, no houses, and no sign that anybody had ever been there, except for a palisade of thick tree trunks where the houses had once stood. The bark had been stripped from one of the posts, and carved into the wood in capital letters was the single word CROATOAN.

> palisade = a fence of stakes, especially for defense

What had happened to the colonists? Three years to wait for a much-needed supply ship is a long time. Did everyone starve to death? What did the word CROATOAN mean? Did a war break out? It seems hard to believe, especially since it had been a Croatoan Indian who had been instrumental in establishing peace. What could have gone wrong? Was the word carved as a warning?

> instrumental = helpful

No, thought White. It must be a message, and he believed—or at least hoped—he would find all the settlers safe and sound on Croatoan Island. But a rising storm prevented them from sailing, so they decided to head to the West Indies, pick up water and supplies, and then return. But that was not to be either. The ship was blown far off course, and despite all their intentions, they never again returned to Roanoke. To this day, the fate of the colonists remains a mystery.

Go On

8 It is likely that the colonists could have gotten along better with the Native Americans on Roanoke if the colonists had

- **F** understood the Native American's way of life
- **G** paid for the fish traps and food the Native Americans gave them
- **H** immediately helped the Native Americans with farming
- **J** attempted to live in the Native American villages

Tip: To predict possible outcomes, think about what the people or characters expect from one another. In this question, clue words such as "could have gotten along better" can lead you to the reason for the conflict.

9 Read this sentence from the passage:

Trees had to be chopped down, all the bricks for their house had to be formed and baked, and a forge had to be built so they could manufacture nails.

In this sentence, what does *forge* mean?

- **A** falsify a document
- **B** an alliance between countries
- **C** push ahead through difficulties
- **D** a furnace to heat metal

Tip: To find the meaning of an unknown word, try to determine its part of speech. Reread the sentence above to determine whether "forge" is a noun, a verb, an adjective, or another part of speech. When you have determined the part of speech, reread the answer choices to find the correct one.

10 According to the passage, how did the colony on Roanoke Island begin?

- **F** Native Americans migrated there from North Carolina.
- **G** People from the West Indies went there for supplies and decided to stay.
- **H** Elizabeth I gave permission to establish a colony there.
- **J** Manteo invited citizens of England to live there.

Tip: To find details in a passage, identify key words in each answer choice and skim the passage for those words and words that are related to them. Choose the answer choice that clearly explains the start of the Roanoke colony and who or what was responsible for its start.

11 Compared to the Native Americans described in the passage, the first colonists on Roanoke

- **A** were not strong enough to swim to Croatoan
- **B** did not know how to make everything they needed
- **C** ate larger meals in the morning and evening
- **D** sang English songs loudly

Tip: When asked to compare and contrast, sketch a Venn diagram. A Venn diagram uses two overlapping circles. You can use it to write details that show how two topics are alike and different. Make a Venn diagram for settlers and Native Americans. Use details from paragraphs 2 and 3.

New York State English Language Arts Standards
8. (1) **Read for information and understanding.** Draw conclusions and make inferences.
9. (1) **Read for information and understanding.** Use text to understand vocabulary.
10. (1) **Read for information and understanding.** Use knowledge of structure, content, and vocabulary to understand informational text.
11. (1) **Read for information and understanding.** Compare and contrast information.

New York State

12 What was probably the author's purpose in writing this passage?

- F to prove that the English colonized Croatoan
- G to tell an interesting story about an unsolved mystery
- H to teach people the value of working together
- J to offer a comparison of Roanoke and Plymouth Rock

Tip: Most passages are written to inform, to persuade, or to entertain. Reread the first and last paragraph of the passage to help determine which of these the passage most likely attempts to accomplish.

13 According to the passage, which of the following is an opinion?

- A Elizabeth I gave Sir Walter Raleigh permission to establish a colony along the shore of what is now North Carolina.
- B Three years to wait for a much-needed supply ship is a long time.
- C On board was Governor John White, whose daughter had just given birth.
- D More than thirty years before the Pilgrims landed at Plymouth Rock, an English colony was founded on Roanoke Island.

Tip: An opinion is something that someone believes. It cannot be checked because opinions are neither correct nor incorrect. Facts, on the other hand, can be proved. Read each answer choice and determine whether it can be proved correct or incorrect.

14 The author of the passage shows that bad timing contributed to the downfall of Roanoke Island by

- F describing events that occurred in chronological order
- G using short sentences that describe Raleigh and the colonists
- H including details about the war, the boat accident, and the storm
- J writing paragraphs that contain unnecessary details

Tip: When asked to find an example of a concept, brainstorm a few ideas on your own before searching through a passage. For example, bad timing might result in missing the school bus or reaching the telephone just as it stops ringing. Skim the passage again, looking for events that prevented other events.

Go On

New York State English Language Arts Standards
12. (3) **Read for critical analysis and evaluation.** Identify author's purpose.
13. (3) **Read for critical analysis and evaluation.** Distinguish between fact and opinion.
14. (3) **Read for critical analysis and evaluation.** Identify author's techniques.

Modeled Instruction: Reading 2

DIRECTIONS: In this part of the test, you are going to read a poem called "A Proper Place" and an article called "The Delicate Balance." You will answer questions and write about what you have read. You may look back at the poem and the article as often as you like.

A Proper Place

by Robert Nye

Outside my window
two tall witch-elms
toss their inspired
green heads in the sun
and lean together
whispering.
Trees make the world
A proper place.

12 • Modeled Instruction

New York State

15 How does the poet use personification in this poem? Use details from the poem to support your answer.

_____
_____
_____
_____
_____
_____

> 🌀 **Tip:** Personification is a description that gives human qualities to nonhuman things. Read the poem again, and look for verbs that usually describe human actions.

16 In the chart below, write the clues that show the time and place in which the poem is set. Then interpret the clues.

Clue Words	What the Clue Words Mean
Place	Place
Time	Time

> 🌀 **Tip:** Setting is not always stated clearly in a poem. Remember that *time* can mean summer or September, but it can also mean ten o'clock or mid-afternoon. Place can also mean somewhere specific, such as Albany, but it can also mean something particular to one person, such as "on my back porch." Find clue words in the poem that help you identify setting.

Go On

New York State English Language Arts Standards
15. (3) **Read and write for critical analysis and evaluation.** Identify author's techniques.
16. (1) **Read and write for critical analysis and evaluation.** Interpret setting.

Modeled Instruction • 13

The Delicate Balance
from Our Global Greenhouse

by April Koral

Greenhouses can be found in botanical gardens and plant nurseries. They are used to grow flowers, plants, fruits, and vegetables. The roof of a greenhouse is made of glass. So are the sides.

If you've ever been in a greenhouse, what you probably remember most about it was how warm it was. The reason the air is so warm inside a greenhouse is that the glass lets the heat from the sun in, but prevents most of the heat from escaping back out. The heat trapped inside is used to help grow plants that thrive in warm climates.

Like a greenhouse, the earth is warmed by the sun. Sunlight striking the surface of the earth is converted to heat. Most of this heat escapes back into space. But today more of it is being trapped in the earth's atmosphere. Because of the resemblance to the way heat is trapped in a greenhouse, scientists call this trend toward increased global warming the greenhouse effect.

The earth's average temperature has only rarely gone up or down more than three or four degrees Fahrenheit in the last ten thousand years. But scientists say that because of the greenhouse effect, our weather may change more in the next decade than it has in tens of thousands of years.

They predict that the earth will become hotter. In some parts of the world, winters will be warmer, while summers will be hotter. There will be more rainfall in the tropics of South America and Southeast Asia, where it already rains a great deal. In other places, such as in Egypt and areas of Africa where people often go hungry because there is not enough water to grow food, there may be even less rain.

The greenhouse effect will probably also change the weather of the United States. In Iowa, for example, there may no longer be enough rain to grow corn, and in Dallas, Texas, the temperature might soar to over 100 degrees Fahrenheit for seventy-eight days a year, instead of the nineteen days it now hits the 100 degree mark.

Another possible result of the greenhouse effect will be that the world's oceans will rise, probably by one to four feet during the next century. As the oceans rise, levels of salt in inland and underground waterways will increase, endangering freshwater fish and contaminating drinking supplies! Beaches and ports may be washed away by the water. Along the coasts of Louisiana, Texas, and Florida, many people might have to move from their homes.

A few scientists believe that some of these changes have already begun. We have been keeping temperature records for a hundred years or so. Four of the last ten years have been the hottest since records began. And 1988 was the warmest year of all.

Why is this happening? Our planet is a delicate balance of natural forces. It is like a clock that never needs to be rewound or have its battery changed. It should just keep on ticking, unless we disturb the balance. This is what scientists say has been happening. We have been disturbing the balance of gases in the earth's atmosphere.

The atmosphere is the blanket of air that surrounds the earth and protects us from the sun's harshest rays. It contains mostly nitrogen (about 80 percent by volume) and oxygen (about 20 percent). There are also small amounts of many other gases. One of these gases is carbon dioxide.

Carbon dioxide plays an important role in living things. Animals and people breathe in oxygen and use it for energy and growth. Carbon dioxide is created in the process and breathed out as a waste product. Plants take in this carbon dioxide and make food with it, through the process of photosynthesis. They give off oxygen as a waste product. This is the oxygen we breathe in.

The amount of carbon dioxide in a planet's atmosphere affects the temperature on that planet! The earth has just the right amount of carbon dioxide in its atmosphere for life to thrive. In most parts of the planet, it is not too hot or too cold, and humans can live quite comfortably and raise food to eat.

Carbon dioxide exists naturally in the atmosphere in small quantities. But it is also produced every time we burn something that contains carbon. Carbon is in the so-called fossil fuels—coal, oil, and natural gas. We use these fossil fuels all the time—to run factories, power plants (which make electricity), cars, trucks, and buses. We also use them to heat our homes. Each time we burn a fossil fuel, more and more carbon dioxide floats up into the atmosphere. Right now the people of the world are putting more than 5.5 billion tons of carbon, in the form of carbon dioxide gas, into the atmosphere every year. Seventy-five percent of this amount comes from the burning of fossil fuels. The destruction of forests accounts for most of the rest. As more and more carbon dioxide builds up in the atmosphere, less heat can escape, and the planet gets hotter.

Other gases are also trapping the planet's heat. These include chlorofluorocarbons (CFCs), methane, and nitrous oxide. Like carbon dioxide, some of these other greenhouse gases, including methane and nitrous oxide, have been in our planet's atmosphere for a long time. But we are now producing them in much larger amounts than ever before. Others, such as CFCs, are relatively new and made only in factories and laboratories.

This tremendous increase in the quantities of greenhouse gases has upset the atmosphere's delicate balance. The result may be the most serious environmental problem this planet has ever faced.

Go On

17 How is the earth's changing climate similar to that of a greenhouse? Use information from "The Delicate Balance" in your answer.

_____

_____

_____

_____

_____

_____

> **Tip:** When asked to compare two things, first jot down the qualities of each of them. Think about the qualities of a greenhouse. Look for details in the article that describe Earth's climate in similar ways. Use a list to organize the details you find.

New York State English Language Arts Standard
17. (1) Read and write for information and understanding. Compare and contrast information.

Modeled Instruction

Planning Page

You may PLAN your writing for Number 18 here if you wish, but do NOT write your final answer on this page. Your writing on this Planning Page will NOT count toward your final score. Write your final answer on Pages 18 and 19.

Tip: Write an outline, create a web, or make notes to help you organize your ideas and plan your writing.

Answer →

Modeled Instruction

18 Compare and contrast the attitude toward nature that is expressed in Robert Nye's poem, "A Proper Place" with the concerns about the environment expressed by April Koral in "A Delicate Balance." Use information from BOTH passages to support your answer.

In your answer, be sure to include:
- the "message" of Nye's poem
- the main ideas of Koral's article
- details from BOTH the poem and the article

Check your writing for correct spelling, grammar, and punctuation.

_____
_____
_____
_____
_____
_____
_____
_____
_____
_____
_____
_____
_____
_____

Tip: To explain why a writer makes certain points, try to identify why he or she wrote the passage. Skim the poem and article, jotting down words, phrases, and sentences that express how the writer really feels about the environment.

New York State English Language Arts Standard
18. (3) **Read and write for critical analysis and evaluation.** Use critical analysis to evaluate ideas.

18 • Modeled Instruction

Go On

Modeled Instruction: Listening

DIRECTIONS: In this section, you will listen to two articles: "Mae Jemison" and "The Past, Present, and Future of Mars." Then you will answer some questions to show how well you understood what was read.

You will listen to the articles twice. As you listen carefully, you may take notes on the articles anytime you wish during the readings. You may use these notes to answer the questions that follow. Use the space on Pages 21 and 22 for your notes.

These articles are about scientific discovery. They deal with the ways science helps increase human knowledge. Here are names included in the articles that may be unfamiliar to you:

- Mae Jemison
- Peace Corps
- The Jemison Group, Inc.
- Jemison Institute for Advancing Technology in Developing Countries
- Percival Lowell
- NASA

Tip: Listen carefully for main ideas and details. In your notes, answer the questions *who, what, when, where, why,* and *how*. Write short phrases instead of complete sentences.

Notes

"Mae Jemison"

Notes

"The Past, Present, and Future of Mars"

19 In the chart below, describe one way that Mae Jemison and taking pictures of Mars' surface inspire people to become more interested in science.

Scientist	Scientific Event
Mae Jemison	Taking pictures of Mars' surface
Inspiration to Others	Inspiration to Others

Tip: Review your listening notes to find details about Jemison and the Mars pictures. In the graphic organizer, mention one reason Jemison and the scientific event inspire people to be interested in science.

20 The article "Mae Jemison" attributes this idea to Jemison:

People should never limit themselves—even if other people have limited imaginations.

Use information from "Mae Jemison" to explain what the quotation means and why Jemison held this view.

_____
_____
_____
_____

Tip: Look at your notes to find how you know Jemison draws from her own experiences in this quotation.

Go On

New York State English Language Arts Standards
19. (3) **Listen and write for critical analysis and evaluation.** Use critical analysis to evaluate information.
20. (3) **Listen and write for critical analysis and evaluation.** Use critical analysis to evaluate information.

21 How does space exploration remain an influence in today's world? Use information from both articles to support your answer.

_____

_____

_____

_____

_____

_____

> 💡 **Tip:** Review your listening notes to find examples of programs or interests that are still underway.

New York State English Language Arts Standard
21. (3) **Write for critical analysis and evaluation.** Use critical analysis to evaluate information.

Planning Page

You may PLAN your writing for Number 22 here if you wish, but do NOT write your final answer on this page. Your writing on this Planning Page will NOT count toward your final score. Write your final answer on Pages 26 and 27.

Tip: Listening notes can help you plan an essay. Use your notes from Pages 21 and 22 to help you plan and write your essay.

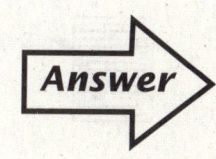

Answer →

22. Describe what might happen if Mae Jemison were to meet a young person who is interested in science and who does not think scientific proof that life on Mars exists is needed. Instead, the person believes that life on Mars exists because as he or she says, "There is life on Earth, so there must also be life on Mars."

In your answer, be sure to include
- examples of what the young person might say
- examples of what Jemison might say
- information from BOTH articles

✓ Check your writing for correct spelling, grammar, and punctuation.

___

Tip: Use details about a person's life to draw conclusions about him or her. The events of Jemison's life show that she is a very encouraging person but that she is also a serious scientist. Review your listening notes to find examples of both of these traits. Then think about what she might say to this young person.

New York State English Language Arts Standard
22. (3) **Write for critical analysis and evaluation.** Use critical analysis to evaluate information.

Planning Page

You may PLAN your writing for Number 23 here if you wish, but do NOT write your final answer on this page. Your writing on this Planning Page will NOT count toward your final score. Write your answer on Pages 29, 30 and 31.

> **Tip:** Choose a single event for your story. Do not tell more than one story. Create a web before you begin writing. Include the people, setting, and details about the event in the web.

Answer →

Modeled Instruction

Modeled Instruction: Writing

23. The passage "The Past, Present, and Future of Mars" tells about how people have always wanted to believe that there is life on Mars. Write about a time when you found out that something you wanted to believe was true turned out not to be true.

In your story, be sure to include
- a description of the setting
- names of other people
- details about the event

Check your writing for correct spelling, grammar, capitalization, and punctuation.

___

Tip: When you are writing about something that really happened, imagine that your reader knows nothing about you or the event. This will remind you to write descriptively. Even if you have seen the place where your story is set thousands of times, try to write about it in a way that someone who has never been there can "see" the place. Include details about the other senses as well so that the reader can experience the story as fully as possible.

Go On

New York State English Language Arts Standard
23. (1) Write for information and understanding. Draw conclusions and make inferences.

Test-Taking Tips

Now you are ready to try the Practice Test for the New York State English Language Arts Test. Use what you learned in the first section of this book to help you do well on the test. If you become familiar with the way the real test looks and the kinds of questions you will answer, you will be better prepared and more relaxed when you take the real test.

Remember these hints when you are taking the test.

- Listen carefully to the directions. Be sure to read all of the directions in the practice test section. Ask your teacher to explain any directions you do not understand.

- Read each selection carefully. Then read each question carefully. As you answer the questions, you may look back at the reading selections as often as you like.

- Listen carefully when a selection is read to you. Try to imagine the setting, characters, and action of the story as you listen. Take notes that will help you answer the questions after you have heard the story. Look back at your notes as often as you like when you answer questions about the story.

- Plan your time. You may want to glance quickly through the entire session before you begin answering questions in order to make the best use of the time you have.

- When you take the practice test, you will answer multiple-choice questions on a separate Answer Sheet. Fill in the answer bubbles completely. If you change your answer, be sure to erase your first answer completely.

- When you answer the open-ended questions, be sure to include details from the reading or listening selections to support your answers. You will write your answers in this book in the spaces provided.

- When you see this symbol, be sure to check your writing for correct spelling, grammar, capitalization, and punctuation.

To get the highest score on the open-ended questions, remember to

✔ organize and express your ideas clearly

✔ answer the question completely

✔ support your ideas with examples

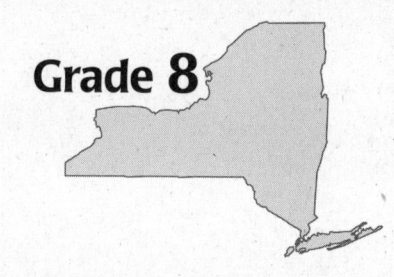

Grade 8 New York State Testing Program

English Language Arts Book 1

Session 1

Part 1

Directions

The following article describes the novelist Robert Cormier and his fans. Read "The Monster as Clark Kent" by Patricia J. Campbell. Then do Numbers 1 through 5.

The Monster as Clark Kent

by Patricia J. Campbell

The man who has just opened the door is Robert Cormier. This is the writer who has been called one of the finest unsung novelists in America today. *The New York Times Book Review* described him, quite accurately, as "the picture of a small-city newspaperman—slight, sort of wispy, gray; a man who's reported the fires and Lions Club meetings and courthouse corruption. He's also a nice man, a family man . . ." They forgot to say that his eyes gaze straight at you with kindly frankness from behind his big glasses and that his ears are endearingly large. He doesn't look like a man who writes novels of stunning impact about the monstrous and inexorable power of evil. He looks like Clark Kent.

paradox = contradiction

He himself recognizes the paradox. He has written: "Look at me: I cry at sad novels, long for happy endings, delight in atrocious puns, pause to gather branches of bittersweet at the side of a highway. I am shamelessly sentimental—I always make a wish when I blow out the candles on my birthday cake, and I dread the day when there may be no one there to say 'Bless you' when I sneeze . . . I hesitate to kill a fly, but people die horrible deaths in my novels."

"These are terrifying times," he muses. "I'm terrified half the time. The strange thing is, basically I'm an optimistic person."

His sunny compassion shows up in innumerable small ways. If you ask how to pronounce his name (Is it Cor-MEER? Cor-mee-AY?) he will assure you that the version you have just used is fine, and the way most people say it. But overheard speaking unaware on the phone, he introduces himself as Bob COR-mee-ehr. About to visit a junior high school class, he was warned by the teacher in the hall that the students had been very impressed by the dark aspects of his books and were expecting some sort of monster to walk through the door. So he deliberately tripped as he crossed the threshold, to make himself look silly and to disarm their fears.

Go On

Cormier has confessed that Adam Farmer in *I Am the Cheese* is a character that comes close to being autobiographical, not in the events of the story but in the fears and phobias that torment him. Like Adam, Cormier suffers from migraines. "The old drill right here," he says, pointing to his temple. Also like Adam, he is afraid of dogs. "When I was a kid I was chased by a thousand dogs on my paper route. I'm still not that comfortable with them, big ones especially and small ones on certain occasions."

... The daily events of his life are peaceful. For twenty-three years he has lived in the same two-story shingled house in a pleasant wooded suburb of Leominster. Here he and his wife, Connie, have raised four children. All are now married and live not too far away. His modest beige Volvo sedan stands in the driveway. The living room has big soft chairs, a snug window seat, a baby grand piano that was given years ago to Connie's mother by her father (a spectacular gift in the Depression and an incident that Cormier has used in at least two stories). Several shelves hold tokens and mementos from fans, in the shape of ceramic beehives or plastic school buses or homemade miniature bicycles.

At one end of the dining room is a small alcove that is Cormier's study—the magic phone booth where Clark Kent rips off his jacket to become Superman. Among the clutter of books and papers is a stereo console, and near the desk is his battered standard reporter's manual Royal typewriter. (At one point he had traded it in for a new electric, but in a few days he went back and retrieved his old friend at a financial loss—much to the shopkeeper's bafflement.) Here in this office without a door Cormier "weaves his writing into the fabric of his existence," as he has said, always available to his family. His years as a newsman have made him immune to noise and distraction when he works.

... Cormier's rapport with his own and other young adults has made him extremely open and available to his readers. In *Catcher in the Rye*, Holden Caulfield says, after finishing Isak Dinesen's *Out of Africa*, "What really knocks me out is a book that, when you're all done reading it, you wish the author that wrote it was a terrific friend of yours and you could call him up on the phone whenever you felt like it." Cormier is that kind of author. Teenagers can call him up anytime: it is a well-known secret that Amy Hertz's phone number in *I Am the Cheese* is Cormier's own. His readers do call, often.

Letters pour in, too, from readers who want to find out why a certain character did what, or the meaning of a puzzling turn in the plot. Typically, boys ask about *The Chocolate War* and girls have questions about *I Am the Cheese*, although there are exceptions. The intricate last chapter of *I Am the Cheese* has drawn so many questions that a class at Fitchburg State College has prepared an answer sheet for Cormier to mail out, revealing the enlightening nuggets of plot facts that can be ferreted out of earlier chapters. But usually he feels that a thoughtful question deserves a personal answer, sometimes as long as two closely written sheets. It distresses him when he finds that a correspondent has forgotten to include a return address, or worse, has written it only on the envelope—which Cormier has already thrown away. He values the discipline of this feedback from his audience highly: "They keep me sharp. They ask some very tough questions about things I haven't really thought through."

> ferreted = found by searching

1 Which of the following statements is an opinion?

- **A** Like Adam, Cormier suffers from migraines.
- **B** So he deliberately tripped as he crossed the threshold, to make himself look silly and to disarm their fears.
- **C** For twenty-three years he has lived in the same two-story shingled house.
- **D** He's also a nice man.

2 Read this sentence from the article:

Cormier's rapport with his own and other young adults has made him extremely open and available to his readers.

In this sentence, what does *rapport* mean?

- **F** secret meeting
- **G** writing style
- **H** close relationship
- **J** enthusiasm

3 According to what you have read, Robert Cormier can be compared to Clark Kent because

- **A** they both wear dark glasses
- **B** they both work as newspaper reporters
- **C** Cormier compared himself to Clark Kent in a previous interview
- **D** Cormier is a mild man who is concerned about the power of evil

4 Why does Cormier encourage his readers to ask him questions about his work?

- **F** He wants to be the kind of author that Holden Caulfield talks about.
- **G** He wants them to continue to read his books.
- **H** He finds that it helps him think about his writing more carefully.
- **J** He does not like to disappoint anyone.

5 Read this sentence from the article:

He doesn't look like a man who writes novels of stunning impact about the monstrous and inexorable powers of evil.

In this sentence, what does the word *inexorable* mean?

- **A** formal
- **B** unstoppable
- **C** inhuman
- **D** historical

Go On

Session 1: Part 1

Directions

Read this excerpt from "The Raven" by Edgar Allan Poe. Then do Numbers 6 through 10.

from The Raven
by Edgar Allan Poe

Once upon a midnight dreary, while I pondered, weak and weary,
Over many a quaint and curious volume of forgotten lore,
While I nodded, nearly napping, suddenly there came a tapping,
As of someone gently rapping, rapping at my chamber door.
"Tis some visitor," I muttered, "tapping at my chamber door;
Only this and nothing more."

lore = tradition or beliefs

Ah, distinctly I remember it was in the bleak December,
And each separate dying ember wrought its ghost upon the floor.
Eagerly I wished the morrow; vainly I had sought to borrow
From my books surcease of sorrow, sorrow for the Lost Lenore,
For the rare and radiant maiden whom the angels name Lenore,
Nameless here for ever more.

surcease = stop

And the silken, sad, uncertain rustling of each purple curtain
Thrilled me—filled me with fantastic terrors never felt before;
So that now, to still the beating of my heart, I stood repeating
"'Tis some visitor entreating entrance at my chamber door,
Some late visitor entreating entrance at my chamber door.
This it is and nothing more."

Presently my soul grew stronger; hesitating then no longer,
"Sir," said I, "or Madam, truly your forgiveness I implore;
But the fact is I was napping, and so gently you came rapping,
And so faintly you came tapping, tapping at my chamber door,
That I scarce was sure I heard you." Here I opened wide the door—
Darkness there and nothing more.

Deep into that darkness peering,
   long I stood there wondering, fearing,
Doubting, dreaming dreams
   no mortal ever dared to dream before;
But the silence was unbroken,
   and the stillness gave no token,
And the only word there spoken
   was the whispered word, "Lenore!"
This I whispered, and an echo
   murmured back the word, "Lenore!"—
Merely this, and nothing more.

38 • Practice Test

Session 1: Part 1

6 Which excerpt from the poem uses a metaphor, the literary technique that directly compares two things?

- **F** "Deep into that darkness peering"
- **G** "filled me with fantastic terrors"
- **H** "dying ember wrought its ghost upon the floor"
- **J** "Once upon a midnight dreary, while I pondered"

7 The speaker's late-night visitor in this poem represents

- **A** family
- **B** failure
- **C** gratitude
- **D** memory

8 Why is the speaker staying awake late reading?

- **F** He is cheerful and carefree.
- **G** He is lonely and sorrowful.
- **H** He is young and strong.
- **J** He is angry and aggressive.

9 They style and wording of the poem show that the poet is

- **A** entertaining the reader by telling a mysterious tale
- **B** persuading the reader not to answer the door late at night
- **C** informing the reader about the speaker's life
- **D** describing the speaker's home

10 Which statement best expresses the main idea of the poem?

- **F** Too much time alone can make a person hear things.
- **G** It is always cold and dreary in December.
- **H** Losing a loved one can have serious emotional effects.
- **J** Lenore was not a real person.

Go On

Session 1: Part 1

Directions

Read this article from 1998 about a small town in Ohio. Then do Numbers 11 through 15.

Ohio Town Finding Future in Historic Civil War Past

THE ASSOCIATED PRESS Ripley, Ohio—Five years after this scenic Ohio River village lost its biggest employer, the town is finding rebirth in its abolitionist past.

> abolitionist = someone who opposes slavery

Just about every family in Ripley was affected when the U.S. Shoe factory closed in 1993, eliminating four hundred jobs.

"My mother and father worked there, and all my friends' mothers and fathers worked there," said former Mayor Roddy Scott, 52. "It was the end of an era when that factory closed."

But the village of 1,800 has regrouped in part by showcasing its legacy as a station on the Underground Railroad, the network of hiding places and safehouses where fugitive slaves were shepherded to freedom in the North.

Author Harriet Beecher Stowe found inspiration in stories she heard from the fervent abolitionists here. In her book, *Uncle Tom's Cabin*, the fleeing slave Eliza walked across the frozen Ohio River to freedom in Ripley.

Several brick houses from that era remain, having endured the yearly flooding that occurred until a series of dams was built between Pittsburgh and Cincinnati. Some of the homes, with views of the Kentucky hills, have been restored as bed-and-breakfast inns for people exploring Underground Railroad routes. The homes of abolitionist John Rankin and freedman John Parker, an entrepreneur and inventor, are both listed as National Historic landmarks.

> entrepreneur = a person who manages a business

"Travel and tourism—that seems to be where our future is leading," said Hilda Frebis, the clerk-treasurer of Ripley.

Session 1: Part 1

Many residents now drive to factories in Cincinnati or car plants in Kentucky to make a living. People who grew up here don't want to leave, and retirees who became familiar with the area while boating or camping are moving in.

"Ripley just decided to rebound from this blow rather than roll over and play dead," said village historian Betty Campbell. "We made the best of it."

U.S. Shoe paid to retrain workers, and government grants—about $2-million worth, Frebis said—let the village pour new concrete curbs and build red brick crosswalks.

"A lot of good things have come out of the closing," said Phil White, a life-long resident. "It was hard on a lot of people at first, but a lot of neat things are going on now. That really was a wake-up call."

White is betting Ripley will survive. He helped restore two historic homes that date to the 1820s.

He treasures the familiarity of Ripley, and he's proud that his daughter is the fifth generation to live in the house where he grew up.

"I like the people," White said. "I know everybody. When you have deep roots, it's hard to leave. I want to bring up my daughter here."

Main Street in Ripley

11 It is likely that the leaders of other small towns that have lost major employers will

A try to get U.S. Shoe to open factories there
B encourage people to move away
C consider new ways to attract visitors
D install new sidewalks and curbs

12 Why did people consider the closing of the shoe factory in Ripley to be important?

F Most of the residents moved away.
G Some residents restored their homes as bed-and-breakfast inns.
H People had to travel long distances to find new jobs.
J The residents were forced to change their lifestyles.

13 According to what you have read, the mayor probably says, "It was the end of an era when that factory closed" in order to show that

A no one was interested in seeing Underground Railroad sites
B methods of manufacturing shoes had changed
C many generations of Ripley citizens had worked in the factory
D it was the last factory dating from the Civil War years

14 The people of Ripley believe tourists will visit their town mainly because it

F is the site of a Civil War battlefield
G has many campgrounds and recreational areas
H offers places for visitors to go boating on the Ohio River
J was once a station on the Underground Railroad

15 The Ohio River was important during the Civil War because

A it marked the boundary between slave and free states
B fugitive slaves were smuggled into Cincinnati by boat
C it often flooded, preventing soldiers from crossing it
D it was a major shipping lane for the Underground Railroad

Directions

Look at the Web page for an Internet site offering services to skateboard owners. Then do Numbers 16 through 18.

How To Protect Your Skateboard

- Register
- How It Works
- Police Protection
- Licensing Your Skateboard
- Skateboard News
- About NYSR

The New York Skateboard Registry—NYSR
Did you know that many missing skateboards are actually stolen, not just misplaced? Many of the stolen decks are eventually found by the police. With our excellent program, you can register your skateboard with us and help protect it against theft. We put each skateboard's registration number in our electronic system, and we match them with police reports of recovered skateboards. If your deck is stolen and later recovered by police officers, we will contact you.

Registering Your Skateboard
You can register online using our Web site. Or you can register by printing out a registration form found on our Web site. Just complete the form and mail it to the address listed on the form. There is a $10 yearly fee, payable by check or credit card.

Registration Supplies
When we receive your registration form and fee, we will send you a document that shows your registration number. Your statement of registration will prove that you are the owner of the skateboard in the event that you need to claim it.

Last Name: [ ] First Name: [ ]
Address: [ ] Phone*: [ ]
City: [ ] E-mail: [ ]
State: [ ] Zip Code: [ ] Web Site*: [ ]
Skateboard Model: [ ] Registration Number: [ ]

*Optional

If you would like more information about our service or any other participating organization, please click the appropriate link below.

Affiliated Law Enforcement Agencies

Affiliated Retailers

Affiliated Web Sites

NYSR Brochures

NYSR "Don't Let Thieves Take Your Skateboard" Poster

■ Clear form and start over.   ■ Submit information to NYSR.   ■ Print form.

Go On

Session 1: Part 1

16 The service provided by this Web site is mainly intended to

- **F** assist victims of skateboard theft
- **G** tell stories about finding stolen skateboards
- **H** identify popular skateboard models
- **J** describe how to do skateboard tricks

17 This Web site offers skateboard owners

- **A** membership in skateboard clubs
- **B** free skate time at New York State skate parks
- **C** used skateboards for sale
- **D** registration by mail or on the Internet

18 All of the following information is required for registration EXCEPT

- **F** Phone
- **G** Address
- **H** Zip Code
- **J** E-mail

Directions

D.H. Lawrence, a writer of poetry, novels, short stories, plays, essays, and criticism, often wrote about the relationships between people. His stories have been compiled into eight books. Read this excerpt from the story, "Rocking-Horse Winner." Then do numbers 19 through 25.

from Rocking-Horse Winner

by D.H. Lawrence

There was a woman who was beautiful, who started with all the advantages, yet she had no luck. She married for love, and the love turned to dust. She had bonny children, yet she felt they had been thrust upon her, and she could not love them. They looked at her coldly, as if they were finding fault with her. And hurriedly she felt she must cover up some fault in herself. Yet what it was that she must cover up she never knew. Nevertheless, when her children were present, she always felt the center of her heart go hard. This troubled her, and in her manner she was all the more gentle and anxious for her children, as if she loved them very much. Only she herself knew that at the center of her heart was a hard little place that could not feel love, no, not for anybody.

Everybody else said of her: "She is such a good mother. She adores her children." Only she herself, and her children themselves, knew it was not so. They read it in each other's eyes.

There was a boy and two little girls. They lived in a pleasant house, with a garden, and they had discreet servants, and felt themselves superior to anyone in the neighborhood.

Although they had lived in style, they felt always an anxiety in the house. There was never enough money. The mother had a small income, and the father had a small income, but not nearly enough for the social position which they had to keep up. The father went in to town to some office. But though he had good prospects, these prospects never materialized. There was always the grinding sense of the shortage of money, though the style was always kept up.

> materialized = appeared

At last the mother said, "I will see if I can't make something." But she did not know where to begin. She racked her brains, and tried this thing and the other, but could not find anything successful. The failure made deep lines come into her face. Her children were growing up, they would have to go to school. There must be more money, there must be more money. The father, who was always very handsome and expensive in his tastes, seemed as if he would never be able to do anything worth doing. And the mother, who had a great belief in herself, did not succeed any better, and her tastes were just as expensive.

And so the house came to be haunted by the unspoken phrase: There must be more money! There must be more money! The children could hear it all the time, though nobody said it aloud. They heard it at Christmas, when the expensive and splendid toys filled the nursery. Behind the shining, modern rocking horse, behind the smart doll's house, a voice would start whispering: "There must be more money! There must be more money!" And the children would stop playing to listen for a moment. They would look into each other's eyes, to see if they had all heard. And each one saw in the eyes of the other two that they too had heard. "There must be more money! There must be more money!"

It came whispering from the springs of the still-swaying rocking horse, and even the horse, bending his wooden, champion head, heard it. The big doll, sitting so pink and smirking in her new pram, could hear it quite plainly, and seemed to be smirking all the more self-consciously because of it. The foolish puppy, too, that took the place of the Teddy bear, he was looking so extraordinarily foolish for no other reason but that he had heard the secret whisper all over the house: "There must be more money!"

pram = baby carriage

Yet nobody ever said it aloud. The whisper was everywhere, and therefore no one spoke it. Just as no one ever says: "We are breathing!" in spite of the fact that breath is coming and going all the time.

"Mother," said the boy Paul one day, "why don't we keep a car of our own? Why do we always use uncle's or else a taxi?"

"Because we're the poor members of the family," said the mother.

"But why are we, Mother?"

"Well—I suppose," she said slowly and bitterly, "it's because your father has no luck."

The boy was silent for some time.

"Is luck money, Mother?" he asked, rather timidly.

"No, Paul. Not quite. It's what causes you to have money."

"Oh!" said Paul vaguely. "I thought when Uncle Oscar said filthy lucker, it meant money."

"Filthy lucre does mean money," said the mother. "But it's lucre, not luck."

"Oh!" said the boy. "Then what is luck, Mother?"

"It's what causes you to have money. That's why it's better to be born lucky than rich. If you're rich, you may lose your money. But if you're lucky, you will always get more money."

46 • Practice Test

Session 1: Part 1

19 Which excerpt from the story uses personification, the literary technique that gives objects or things human qualities?

A "She married for love and the love turned to dust."

B "They . . . felt themselves superior to anyone in the neighborhood."

C "The big doll . . . seemed to be smirking all the more self-consciously . . ."

D "A voice would start whispering: 'There must be more money! There must be more money!'"

20 The mother's behavior shows that she

F expects to have money without working for it

G has a good heart but is not very intelligent

H cares deeply for her children and is trying to bring them up right

J understands the value of a dollar

21 What happens when Paul begins to ask questions about his family's way of handling money?

A He decides to get a job in order to help afford the things they like.

B His mother blames their problems on bad luck.

C His friends at school tell him the truth about his parents.

D His mother tells him that he has no right to ask such questions.

22 Which excerpt from the story uses irony, the literary technique that reveals that a narrator's or character's intended meaning is the opposite of what he or she actually means?

F They lived in a pleasant house, with a garden, and they had discreet servants, and felt themselves superior to anyone in the neighborhood.

G "Mother, . . . why don't we keep a car of our own? Why do we always use uncle's or else a taxi?" "Because we're the poor members of the family," said the mother.

H The father, who was always very handsome and expensive in his tastes, seemed as if he would never be able to do anything worth doing.

J The mother had a small income, and the father had a small income, but not nearly enough for the social position which they had to keep up.

23 This story is told by a

A first person narrator

B second person narrator

C third person narrator

D fourth person narrator

Go On

Session 1: Part 1

24 Read this sentence from the story:

The house came to be haunted by the unspoken phrase: There must be more money.

In this sentence, what feeling is communicated?

- **F** Fear because the house is haunted by the previous owners.
- **G** Pride because the mother continues to fill the house with things the family does not need.
- **H** Powerlessness because the desire for money controls the family's lives.
- **J** Shame because the shabbiness of their surroundings constantly reminds the family that they are poor.

25 How is the mother in the story different from other people?

- **A** She believes that luck, not hard work, is how people get money.
- **B** She lives in a house with her husband and children.
- **C** She likes to give and receive nice presents during the holidays.
- **D** Her beliefs about other people may or may not be true.

STOP

New York State Testing Program

Grade 8

English Language Arts

Book 2

Name _____

This test will ask you to write about selections you have listened to or read. Your writing will NOT be scored on what you think about what you have read or heard. It WILL be scored on

- clear organization and expression of ideas
- accurate and complete answers
- examples that support your ideas
- interesting and enjoyable writing
- correct use of grammar, spelling, punctuation, and paragraphs

This symbol will remind you to plan and check your writing.

Session 1

Part 2: Listening

Directions

In this part of the test, you will listen to two articles: "Dinetah: Among the Land of the Navajo" and "Life in an Eskimo Village." Then you will answer some questions to show how well you understood what was read.

You will listen to the articles twice. As you listen carefully, you may take notes on the articles anytime you wish during the readings. You may use these notes to answer the questions that follow. Use the space on Pages 52 and 53 for your notes.

These articles are about the ways of life of two groups. These groups learned to use the environment and natural resources and established their own proud cultures. Here are the spellings of words and names included in the articles that may be unfamiliar to you:

- Dinetah
- Kaibeto Plateau
- hominy
- Yupik
- Naskapi
- Cree
- Inuit
- Inupiat

Notes

"Dinetah: Among the Land of the Navajo"

Notes

"Life in an Eskimo Village"

26 In the chart below, describe one way that Navajo life is different from that of non-Navajo people, and one way it is similar. Use information from "Dinetah: Among the Land of the Navajo" in your answer.

Different	Similar

27 In "Dinetah: Among the Land of the Navajo," LeRoy DeJolie states:

> Because of a growing awareness to preserve the heritage that our Navajo ancestors desired for succeeding generations, I see my work more as a mission than a job.

Use information from "Dinetah: Among the Land of the Navajo" to explain what the quotation means and why DeJolie holds this view.

_____
_____
_____
_____
_____

28 How does the natural environment play a role in the way groups of people learn to live in different places? Use information from both articles to support your answer.

_____

_____

_____

_____

_____

_____

Planning Page

You may PLAN your writing for Number 29 here if you wish, but do NOT write your final answer on this page. Your writing on this Planning Page will NOT count toward your final score. Write your final answer on Pages 57 and 58.

Answer →

29 Describe what a dinner visit at a Navajo family celebration and at an Eskimo settlement in the Far North might be like.

In your answer, be sure to include
- features of each home
- a description of the meals
- information from BOTH articles

Check your writing for correct spelling, grammar, and punctuation.

Go On

Session 1: Part 2

Do NOT turn this page until you are told to do so.

STOP

Session 2

Part 1: Reading

Directions

In this part of the test, you are going to read an article called "Against the Tide" and a poem called "Invictus." You will answer questions and write about what you have read. You may look back at the article and poem as often as you like.

Go On

Session 2: Part 1

Against the Tide

It's a funny thing, how ships are named. This one was *Amistad*. It means "friendship" in Spanish, but it was carrying slaves—fifty-three people who had been bought in Cuba and were being shipped to the United States. The year was 1839 and the story is old, but if you really listen, you will still hear it, even today.

There was an uprising, it seems, and as history held its breath, the fifty-three rose up against their kidnappers, ordering that a course be set for Africa. Outmanned and outnumbered, the crew complied and altered the ship's direction.

Had they been better sailors, they might have been able to navigate by the stars. Or perhaps there weren't any stars that night. Perhaps the moon was new or the sky washed featureless and pale gray with thick clouds. But instead of heading south, the *Amistad* drifted to the northeast.

Some time later, the ship was intercepted by an American brig off the coast of Long Island, New York. In a strange interpretation of the events, the fifty-three Africans were taken prisoner and charged with piracy.

Martin Van Buren was president at the time, and he, along with several newspaper editors, felt that the fifty-three Africans should be extradited to Cuba. But it was the abolitionists who cried out for true justice and demanded that the Africans be afforded their civil rights. The case went to trial.

extradited = turned over to another country

abolitionist = someone who opposes slavery

At a hearing in Hartford, Connecticut, a federal district court judge ruled that the Africans were not liable for their actions on board the *Amistad* because they had been illegally enslaved. But only half the battle had been won. The case moved on to the Supreme Court. There, the Africans were defended by former President John Quincy Adams, who was, perhaps, the ideal counsel. Adams was a northerner and had long been opposed to slavery. His passion and common sense, combined with a clever legal mind, made a powerful statement. In arguing for the freedom of the fifty-three men, Adams pointed out that international law prohibited slave trade. Therefore, the men should neither be held in this country nor returned to Cuba, and should be allowed to live as they wished. The Supreme Court agreed, and in 1851 ruled in favor of freedom for all of the men.

The *Amistad* case is a small story, but it is also a big story. It is about greed and ignorance, justice and humanity. And it is about all of us. Even today.

> Forc'd from home, and all its pleasures,
>
> Afric's coast I left forlorn;
>
> To increase a stranger's treasures,
>
> O'er the raging billows borne.
>
> Men from England bought and sold me,
>
> Paid my price in paltry gold;
>
> But, though theirs they have enroll'd me,
>
> Minds are never to be sold.
>
> [From: "The Negro's Complaint" by William Cowper, pub. 1789]

30 How did the *Amistad* case arrive at the Supreme Court? Explain by relating how one event led to another, using details from the article to support your answer.

_____
_____
_____
_____
_____
_____

Invictus

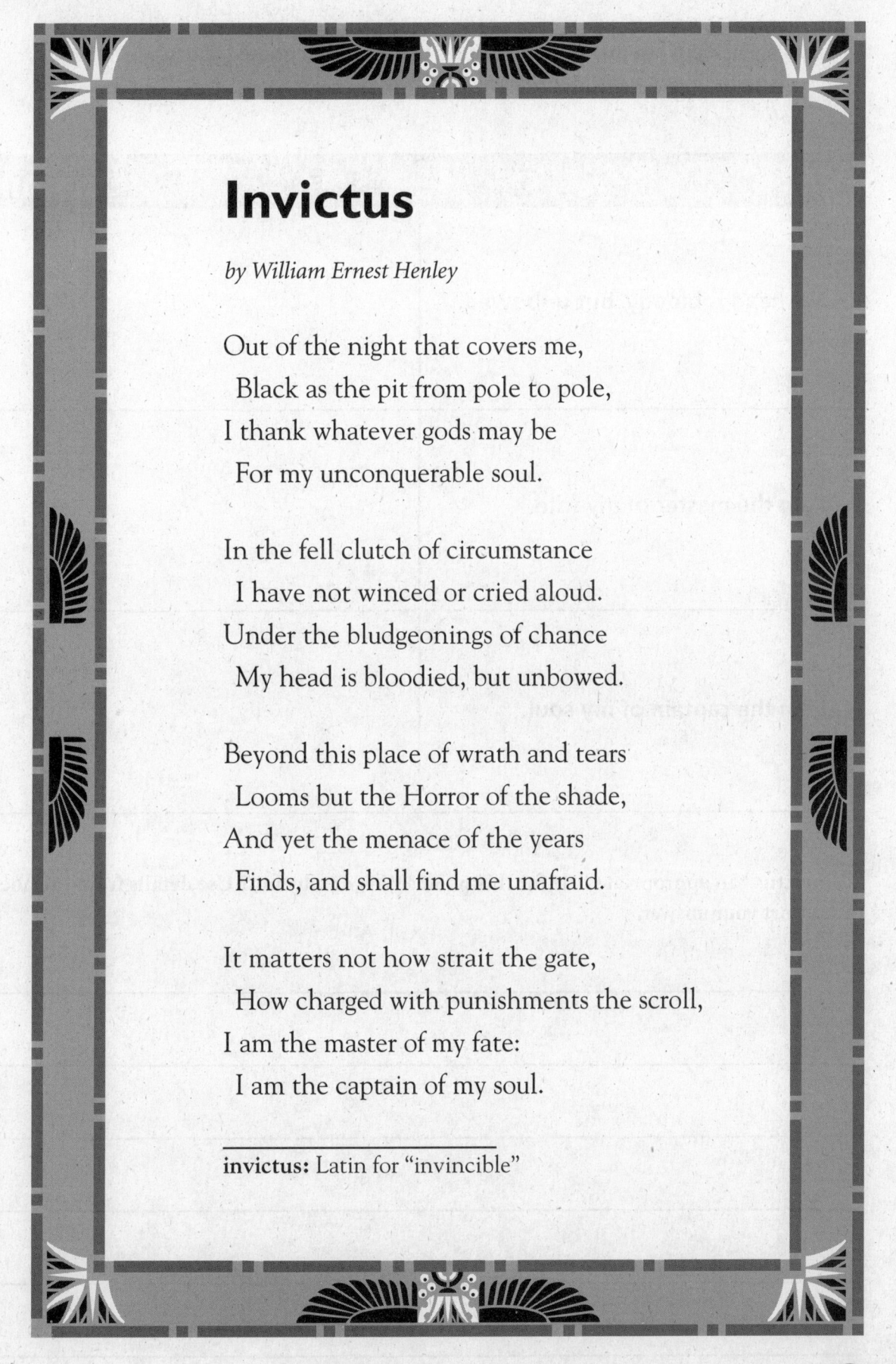

by William Ernest Henley

Out of the night that covers me,
  Black as the pit from pole to pole,
I thank whatever gods may be
  For my unconquerable soul.

In the fell clutch of circumstance
  I have not winced or cried aloud.
Under the bludgeonings of chance
  My head is bloodied, but unbowed.

Beyond this place of wrath and tears
  Looms but the Horror of the shade,
And yet the menace of the years
  Finds, and shall find me unafraid.

It matters not how strait the gate,
  How charged with punishments the scroll,
I am the master of my fate:
  I am the captain of my soul.

---

invictus: Latin for "invincible"

31 Henley's poem has a number of famous lines that are often quoted. Explain what each of these famous lines means in the space provided.

My head is bloody, but unbowed.	
I am the master of my fate.	
I am the captain of my soul.	

32 Is "Invictus" an appropriate title for this poem? Why or why not? Use details from the poem to support your answer.

_____
_____
_____
_____
_____
_____

Go On

Planning Page

You may PLAN your writing for Number 33 here if you wish, but do NOT write your final answer on this page. Your writing on this Planning Page will NOT count toward your final score. Write your final answer on Pages 68 and 69.

Answer →

Go On

Session 2: Part 1

33 Compare and contrast the roles of the slaves on the *Amistad* and that of the speaker of the poem, "Invictus." Use information from BOTH the article and the poem to support your answer.

In your answer, be sure to include
- how the roles were similar
- how they were different
- details from BOTH the article and the poem

Check your writing for correct spelling, grammar, and punctuation.

Session 2

Part 2: Writing

Directions

In this part of the test, you will be writing an original essay. Follow the directions on the next two pages and begin your essay on Page 73.

Planning Page

You may PLAN your writing for Number 34 here if you wish, but do NOT write your final answer on this page. Your writing on this PLANNING PAGE will NOT count toward your final score. Write your final answer on Pages 73 through 75.

34 Since the 1850s, the amount of freedom given to people in America has changed. Write an article for your school newspaper in which you discuss how you think the freedom that people have has changed.

In your answer, be sure to include
- how you think people's freedom has changed
- why you think these changes have occurred
- details to make your writing interesting

Check your writing for correct spelling, grammar, and punctuation.

Answer Sheet

STUDENT'S NAME — LAST, FIRST, MI

SCHOOL:
TEACHER:
FEMALE ○   MALE ○

BIRTH DATE
MONTH	DAY	YEAR
Jan ○	⓪ ⓪	⓪ ⓪
Feb ○	① ①	① ①
Mar ○	② ②	② ②
Apr ○	③ ③	③ ③
May ○	④	④ ④
Jun ○	⑤	⑤ ⑤
Jul ○	⑥	⑥ ⑥
Aug ○	⑦	⑦ ⑦
Sep ○	⑧	⑧ ⑧
Oct ○	⑨	⑨ ⑨
Nov ○		
Dec ○		

GRADE ③ ④ ⑤ ⑥ ⑦ ⑧

Achieve New York State English Language Arts Grade 8

The New York State assessments in English Language Arts are published by CTB/McGraw-Hill. Such company has neither endorsed nor authorized this test-preparation book.

TEST
Book 1, Session 1, Part 1

1 Ⓐ Ⓑ Ⓒ Ⓓ   6 Ⓕ Ⓖ Ⓗ Ⓙ   11 Ⓐ Ⓑ Ⓒ Ⓓ   16 Ⓕ Ⓖ Ⓗ Ⓙ   21 Ⓐ Ⓑ Ⓒ Ⓓ
2 Ⓕ Ⓖ Ⓗ Ⓙ   7 Ⓐ Ⓑ Ⓒ Ⓓ   12 Ⓕ Ⓖ Ⓗ Ⓙ   17 Ⓐ Ⓑ Ⓒ Ⓓ   22 Ⓕ Ⓖ Ⓗ Ⓙ
3 Ⓐ Ⓑ Ⓒ Ⓓ   8 Ⓕ Ⓖ Ⓗ Ⓙ   13 Ⓐ Ⓑ Ⓒ Ⓓ   18 Ⓕ Ⓖ Ⓗ Ⓙ   23 Ⓐ Ⓑ Ⓒ Ⓓ
4 Ⓕ Ⓖ Ⓗ Ⓙ   9 Ⓐ Ⓑ Ⓒ Ⓓ   14 Ⓕ Ⓖ Ⓗ Ⓙ   19 Ⓐ Ⓑ Ⓒ Ⓓ   24 Ⓕ Ⓖ Ⓗ Ⓙ
5 Ⓐ Ⓑ Ⓒ Ⓓ   10 Ⓕ Ⓖ Ⓗ Ⓙ   15 Ⓐ Ⓑ Ⓒ Ⓓ   20 Ⓕ Ⓖ Ⓗ Ⓙ   25 Ⓐ Ⓑ Ⓒ Ⓓ

Book 2, Sessions 1 and 2
Answer open-ended questions directly in the book.